UNEQUALLY YOKED

A Love Story

How to live a victorious life
when the Cross stands between
you and those you love.

Previously titled "Married With{out} Spouses."

Christine M. Carney

UNEQUALLY YOKED

COPYRIGHT © 2010
CHRISTINE CARNEY

ALL RIGHTS RESERVED

Interior layout by Laurie Clark.

Unless otherwise indicated, all Scripture quotations are from the King James Version of the Bible.

ISBN-13 978-0-615-34922-0
First Printing: February 2010

FOR INFORMATION CONTACT:

Christine Carney
3545 Orders Rd.
Grove City, OH 43123

Email me at cmcarney1205@live.com

Printed in the United States of America by

www.instantpublisher.com

ACKNOWLEDGEMENTS

LORD JESUS —Thank you for your Truth, your Salvation and the privilege of being called your daughter.

LYNDA ALLISON DOTY — Your confidence, guidance and Godly example have allowed me to discover my strength and embrace the woman that you saw in me long before I did!

PAT JOHNSON — Thank you for your *capital* editing skills, kind critiques and instant words of encouragement. The way you wield a red pen is like poetry in a ballpoint!

LAURIE CLARK —Your rare artistic talent and *uncanny* ability to produce a complete message from a simple idea— *Rock!* It is an honor to be your sister and a *blessing to have you as a friend.*

THE LOVE OF MY LIFE: RICHARD CARNEY — Thank you for your constant love and support, honey. I am privileged to be your wife and so thankful to share my life with you.

TABLE OF CONTENTS

INTRODUCTION

When I first became a Christian woman married to an unsaved man, I was completely obsessed with my husband's salvation. I felt he must be saved in order to complete my own salvation. My husband's spiritual needs were of paramount importance, far outweighing my need for spiritual growth. His salvation (or the lack, thereof) became invisibly linked and contingent on mine to complete the eternal order of our lives. This type of thinking left me believing that God would not use me until my husband was "in Church."

Does this sound familiar?

Think about it: how many Bible Studies has your husband received? My husband has received at least twice as many as I have, in fact, he probably knows more Bible than me! How many times has a (very well meaning and God bless him) brother asked if he could give your husband a call and maybe meet for breakfast or coffee? And, you have been asked out a few times less.

Over the years, I have spent a lot of time in prayer, fasting and plain old "where-the-rubber-meets-the-road" serving of the Lord. I've struggled, succeeded and fallen flat on my tushie. Without fail, the Lord has been faithful, good and merciful to me. He always reaches down and helps me back up.

During my marriage and my walk with Christ, many challenges have come and gone. I have had trials that have led me through the valley, quiet times when I have meandered through the dell, and hard-won battles that have catapulted me to mountain top experiences. However, the one trial that has stayed with me, like only a faithful thorn in the flesh can, has been my dear husband. You see, he remains unsaved and that fact saddens me beyond words.

In years past, my prayers have been dominated by request after request for my husband. I have tried every angle I can think of to pray. I have prayed specifically, generally, desperately and angrily for God to do something, *anything,* to soften my husband's heart! If I heard a preacher state, "The fervent and effectual prayer of a righteous man..." You can bet my next prayers would be screaming, claiming, and fervent!

When I heard a lesson taught on the woman who constantly bothered the judge until he gave her what she wanted, I would go on a prayer mission. Every other second, I would breathe a prayer for my husband, nonstop, all day, for weeks and weeks and weeks! (I still tend to binge pray for my husband, but the Lord is much more tolerant of me these days.)

My favorite sermon is the one about the Centurion who asks the Lord to heal his daughter, tells the Lord how he understands His authority, Jesus speaks the word of healing, and BAM!—the daughter is healed. Poor Jesus, I would just about wear Him out with my "faith-in-His-authority" prayers!

One day, after a marathon prayer meeting about my husband, I started crying for myself. I was broken, hurt, and tired to the core. I had waited for my husband to become a Christian for twelve years.

I had waited, waited and waited. Sometimes, patiently, other times, not so much. The man was quite content with our life and the status quo. But I, on the other hand, was not at all!

After I had prayed, I blew my nose, straightened myself up and asked the Lord, "How can I ever be effective if I can't even win my own husband?" I started crying again, "if you won't change him, please, Lord, change me." At that moment, the love of Christ swept into the room and wrapped around me in a tender hug. I felt Him say, "Now, we're getting somewhere."

His quiet assurance let me know that I was valued and needed in His kingdom. I sensed His frustration with the road blocks which I have faced every day and the preoccupation I have had with my husband's salvation. All my insecurities began to melt away as the Lord spoke into my heart His plan for my life. God's highest priority for me was to live a victorious and productive life. It was that simple.

Some time passed after this experience, and then, one night on my way to work, I was doing what I normally did: drive and pray. During this prayer time, I came around to my husband's eternal state of affairs. I was still concerned about how I was going to be effective in the kingdom of God. I wanted to be a soul winner, I wanted to reach the lost and encourage those who are struggling. But, how?

"It is BECAUSE of your unsaved husband that you will have a ministry."

The flood gates of understanding opened around me and I began to see the prayers of wives swirl around the throne of God. I saw the women who had waited for 5, 10, 20, or even 30 years for their husbands to give their lives over to Christ. The Lord impressed upon me His love and adoration for us.

Our Father let me know that we are not alone; we have a place in His family and a ministry within the body! Tears of compassion flowed down my cheeks, and I began to feel your heartfelt prayers for your husbands. Soon, my prayers blended with your prayers, and my tears mingled with your tears.

We are called to be the light of the world! It is time for us to take the rightful place God has for women with unsaved husbands in the body of Christ. There is a particular niche for women who are married to unsaved men. But, we must realize our potential and be willing to grow in the Lord, in spite of our circumstance. God has a great job for us and we must believe that we are able to do it. Our focus must turn away from our situation in life and turn toward living a victorious and productive Christian life.

"There was a man [woman] sent from God,

whose name was John [insert your name].

The same came for a witness, to bear witness of the Light, that

all men [your husband] through him might believe. He [She]

was not that Light, but was sent to bear witness of that Light."

John 1:6-8 [brackets mine]

During our time together in this book, you will learn how to live the life of a Christian woman who happens to be married to a non-Christian man. You will come to understand that you are called to serve God and minister as He desires in your life. By the end of our journey, you will be on your way to experiencing spiritual growth and establishing prosperity in your walk in Christ! You will gain confidence to seek, pursue, and fulfill the ministry in which He has called you, to the fullest capacity!

I really, *really* wanted to write a book titled, *Ten Easy Steps Guaranteed to Save Your Unsaved Spouse*, but, I can't. What I can do, is write is a book whose purpose is to share my journey with you, assure you that you are not alone, encourage you to face the day and to be of good cheer!

WHEN LOVE AND SKILL WORK TOGETHER, EXPECT A MASTERPIECE.
~*John Ruskin*

ONCE UPON A TIME

Many years ago, I was on the wilderness journey of a backslider. This is when I met Rich Carney. Ours was not a whirlwind romance, but, a comfortable friendship and a feeling of "home" we had with each other. While we got to know each other, I told him about my background in Pentecost and my desire to "go back to church." In his desire to have me for his bride, Rich showered me with promises of sharing a Christ-centered life with me. In my brain, I understood the error of entertaining the idea of a relationship with Rich. In my heart, I didn't want to be without him.

For many months, I refused Rich's off of marriage. My first experience with marriage left me very cautious about taking another trip down the aisle. The thought of giving my heart to a man and trusting him not to hurt me was foreign. The fear of another failed marriage: not so foreign. But, Rich loved a challenge and he never quit "popping the question."

One morning, Rich asked me to marry him, again. I looked into his soulful Italian eyes and said, "OK. I'll marry you. But, you better make it today, because, if you wait, I might change my mind."

"Get in the Jeep," Rich said as he grabbed his keys. He opened the back door and with a sweep of his hand to show me the way, chuckled, "Let's go."

Within minutes, we were off to Kentucky to get married! Heading south on Interstate 71, I watched the swirl of snowflakes kick up around the Jeep as we drove along the highway. Rich turned on the radio and Christmas music was playing "Silver Bells." I could not keep myself from smiling over at him. His eyes met mine and he asked, "What?"

"The snow and music, honey" I smiled, "It's a good sign."

In what seemed like a blink of an eye, Rich and I were standing in front of a Boone County judge. We were able to round-up two secretaries to stand in as witnesses to our nuptials. I said "I do." Rich said he did. We sealed the marriage with a kiss, shook the Judge's hand and hugged the secretaries' necks.

Done. It took five minutes and cost twenty bucks.

On December 5, 1997, I married Richard Carney. I became Christine Marie Carney and everything else dimmed in comparison! Nothing would ever be the same for either of us. Rich and I had crossed over the point of no return. We were married!

As we walked to the exit, Rich went ahead of me and opened the door, allowing me to go out first. Once we were outside, the brisk winter wind kicked up and bounced us into each other, face to face. I looked up to see Rich smiling at me and felt his arms go around my shoulders.

"I love you, Chris." Rich said. He hugged me away from the cold as we walked to the Jeep.

"I love you, too." I replied, giving him a quick kiss before shivering my way into the passenger seat.

Rich, filled with boyish charm and smiles, jumped into the driver's side. I looked across the seat at the handsome profile of my new husband and thought, "You have no idea what you just got yourself into, buddy."

The following March, I made my way to an altar of repentance and renewed my life in the Lord. After that church service, I went home to Rich a different woman. Real different.

On the way home, I remembered the prenuptial conversations Rich and I had about living a Christ-centered life. When I got home, I found out very quickly that he wasn't thrilled with the change in me. Rich was in a state of shock and I parked myself in a state of denial, trying to convince myself that Rich would come to church with me the following Sunday. Or, next Sunday, or, maybe the next.

Weeks turned into months and Rich never took a real interest in the Lord. When months turned into years, the honeymoon was over. The stress of my children and his children living under the same roof compounded my unrest and discontentedness. I spent most of my time running interference between the exes and children. I was utterly unhappy and I wanted to escape.

I put my nose to the grind stone and started looking for ways out of the marriage. I was miserable, Richard was content. Yes, he told me on more than one occasion, he did want to strangle me, but, he loved me and that would never change. It was me: I wanted out of the mess. I was done being Mrs. Nice Lady and the frill and frou-frou Christian. I was done with the whole marriage thing.

Take the 'L' out of Lover and it's OVER.

This is when I began praying with *great diligence* for a way out of my marriage. I cried out the list of my complaints, one after the other. I pled the blood of Jesus over my situation and ask the Lord to make a way of escape for me. When I married Rich, I was backslidden and not "right." He had to understand I had made a grave mistake. I asked the Lord to forgive my harsh impulsive move. I reminded Him that we had been married in front of a judge. I made sure He understood that that does not count.

I repented again and again, pleading with the Lord for forgiveness and asking for mercy. I knew God was an all merciful God, a forgiver of mistakes, so He would surely let me off the hook. The Lord had to understand that I did not mean to marry Richard. I married him in error. It was a mistake!

Au contraire mon cher. Never, ever, *ever* say that to the Lord. Unless, of course you really, really, *really* enjoy being drug by the scruff of your neck out to the wood shed. Then, get whooped around the wood shed a few times and drug right back to where you started. Hey; if that's how you roll, then, more power to you...and more laps around the wood shed, too. If not, then hear me out on this one and save your hide for another time!

On my most recent trip back to the wood shed, (I never said I learned this lesson the first time!) I may not have heard the voice of God, but, I got the message loud and clear. My Heavenly Father took me by the scruff of my neck and put my nose into some Scripture.

> *For thou, O God, hast heard my vows:*
> *thou hast given me the heritage of those*
> *that fear thy name. Psalms 61:5*

Okay, I admit, I said the vows. God heard me speak the words, "Until death us do part." But, I was not right with God — I was a backslider — I did not have any sense. The vow could not have meant anything, really, since I was not in my right mind? Kind of like, "Not guilty by reason of insanity!" Right?!

I received a firm shake of my scruff.

> *Thou shalt make thy prayer unto him, and he*
> *shall hear thee, and thou shalt pay thy vows.*
> *Job 22:27*

Prayer? I had made prayer. I had made extensive, fervent, continual and unceasing supplication to God! Now, I was expected to pay a vow? There was a price on my marriage vows? Then, what was the twenty bucks for?

> *So will I sing praise unto thy name for ever,*
> *that I may daily perform my vows.*
> *Psalms 61:8*

Lord, are you saying that by praising You, I will be able to perform my vows? All of them? You want me to pay you with praise? Are you serious?

I continued to argue with the Alpha and Omega, the great I AM, the Almighty God, the Prince of Peace about the serious, yet very forgivable error I made in marrying Rich while I was not right with Him.

"Lord, I made a mistake! Please, Forgive me!" I cried.

I felt another firm shake of my scruff.

"When thou vowest a vow unto God, defer not to pay it; for he hath no pleasure in fools: pay that which thou hast vowed. Better is it that thou shouldest not vow, than that thou shouldest vow and not pay. Suffer not thy mouth to cause thy flesh to sin; neither say thou before the angel, that it was an error: wherefore should God be angry at thy voice, and destroy the work of thine hands?"

Ecclesiastes 5:4-6

"Argue with that, Christine Marie." My Father spoke into my heart.

"Oh, no" I thought, "This is *not* in the Bible!"

"Oh, *yes*, it is." The still small voice said with firm authority.

"BUT..."

The voice remained still, small, firm and unruffled, "You can 'but' all you want, Chris. *but*, my Word will never change."

I could not believe that the Lord would put that particular Scripture in the Bible when I was going through such a horrible time in my life. He must have done it while I wasn't looking!

Now, I was on a mission to convince the Lord of my need for freedom. I reread the part of the scripture that said, *"neither say thou before the angel, that it was an error: wherefore should God be angry at thy voice, and destroy the work of thine hands."*

God will be angry at the very sound of my voice? Really? Come ON!

But, angry it says and angry will the Lord be if I continue to call my wedding vows an error, a mistake, a lapse in sanity or a moment of poor judgment. When I married my husband, it may have looked like I was standing in front of a Judge and two secretaries, but, in all reality, I spoke my wedding vows before the Heavenly host of Angels and at the throne of the Most High God. The partaking of marital vows is a sacred act that performs a complete merging of spirit, mind, heart and body which ultimately bears eternal consequences; regardless of where they are spoken.

I realized that I could argue and argue until I was red in the face, but that would not change a thing in the Word. The Lord had finally gotten His point through my thick skull: He does not change. I do.

When we get married, we are verbally signing a marital vow contract with the Lord. Simply stated, being a wife is the act of becoming co-owner and cosigner in our relationship contract. We are responsible for the total amount of the vows owed, regardless of whether or not our husband's make their payment. It is our responsibility to pay the vows we speak and insure that our portion is paid in full, with grace and dignity.

When we make purchases on credit, buy a house or car, interest is applied to the principle of the loan. Bankers will drag out your payments for as long as possible, because the interest of the total amount is paid first. This leaves a mere fraction of the monthly payment being applied to the principle amount, the original amount of money that was borrowed. With each payment, it is wise to pay more than is required and apply it to the principle of the loan. If you do not do this, the debt is not being paid; only the interest.

The nasty loan-shark of our soul would love to keep us

buried in the interest payments and default on our vows. Especially, since he knows that all we have to do is go to our Dad and pay the principle with praise and worship.

IN EVERY MARRIAGE MORE THAN A WEEK OLD, THERE ARE GROUNDS FOR DIVORCE. THE TRICK IS TO FIND, AND CONTINUE TO FIND, GROUNDS FOR MARRIAGE
~Robert Anderson

THE THREE STAGES OF
LOVE AND MARRIAGE:
YOU DON'T KNOW EM,
BUT YOU LOVE EM.
YOU KNOW EM, AND DON'T LOVE EM.
YOU KNOW EM AND YOU LOVE EM.

~Unknown

MARITAL METEOROLOGISTS

"I have no way of knowing whether or not you married the
wrong person, but I do know that many people have a lot of
wrong ideas about marriage and what it takes to make that
marriage happy and successful. I'll be the first to admit that it's
possible that you did marry the wrong person. However, if you
treat the wrong person like the right person, you could well end
up having married the right person after all. On the other hand,
if you marry the right person, and treat that person wrong,
you certainly will have ended up marrying the wrong person. I
also know that it is far more important to be the right kind of
person than it is to marry the right person. In short, whether you
married the right or wrong person is primarily up to you."
~Zig Ziglar

{
Who is a wise man [woman] and
endued with knowledge among you?
Let him shew out of a good conversation
[good manners] his works with
meekness of wisdom.
James 3:13 [brackets mine]

If I had to speak one thing into your heart that would
help you *right now*, it would be this: use good manners with
your spouse. "Please" and "Thank you" reflect love and
appreciation. Treating your husband with kindness and

courtesy not only communicates respect for him, but it speaks volumes about how you feel about yourself. As sure as I am that good manners will strengthen the love in a marriage, I am equally sure that rudeness will destroy it.

> *Likewise, ye wives, be in subjection to your own husbands;*
> *that, if any obey not the word, they also may without the*
> *word be won by the conversation of the wives.*
>
> *1 Peter 3:1*

While studying this Scripture, most of my time was spent on the word *conversation*. I was completely focused on how my husband would be won to the Lord by my conversation, manners or behavior. I chewed on this verse time and time again, praying that the Lord would change me so that my behavior reflected Him. During my studies, the word, *subjection* was secondary, and I didn't give it much thought. In my mind, I read it as another word for submission and put no more thought into it. However, the word *subjection* is the key that unlocks the word *conversation*! It is the tactical logistics of our behavior. For example, *subjection* is like setting up dominoes on edge, in a great design and *conversation* is what happens when we knock the first domino down.

According to Strong's Concordance, *subjection* is from the Greek word *hypotasso:* hypo means beneath or below and *tasso* means "to place in a certain order, to arrange, to assign a place, to appoint mutually, to appoint on one's own responsibility or authority". *Hypotasso* is a social principle of order and decorum for all people. It's an example of how balance and agreement can be kept among the ranks. It is used throughout the Bible as an example of behavior in nature and in mankind. The Lord shows us how to align ourselves with others by applying the principle of subjection in the following Scripture:

> *Let nothing be done through strife or vainglory;*
>
> *but in lowliness of mind let each esteem other better*
>
> *than themselves. Look not every man on his own things,*
>
> *but every man also on the things of others.*
>
> *Philippians 2:3-4*

Back in 1 Peter 3:1, *conversation* is the Greek word *anastrophe*, which means, "manner of life, conduct, behavior, deportment." If you break it down to the root, you'll find the Greek word *trope*, which means "turning, as in the heavenly bodies." Translated, *conversation* means our conduct and behavior can cause a turning of the heavenly bodies, such as clouds or weather. Therefore, it is not unreasonable to assert that, according to scripture, as wives, our conversation will control the emotional and spiritual climate of our home!

So, 1 Peter 3:1 may be read something like this:

> *"Likewise, ye wives, practice the principles of decorum*
> *you have been taught: esteem your own husbands better*
> *than yourself; that, if any obey not the word, they also*
> *may without the word be won by the warm sunshine of a*
> *well placed smile on a cloudy day or by the cool breeze of a*
> *gentle word in the midst of a sweltering heat."*

My husband, Rich works more than an hour away from our home and he loathes traffic. (Actually, he just loathes the other drivers). When he gets home from work, my poor Rich is wound for sound, and if he's had a bad day at work, it is even worse! On these evenings, he is so stressed-out that every word he speaks comes out of his mouth like a bark. Before I understood the concept of subjection and conversation, when Rich would vent his displeasure, I would get bent out of shape and defensive. My disgruntled response to him poured gas on the fire, instead of water. Now, I am more aware of Rich's need to verbalize his feelings and his need for me to simply listen (*subjection*) and give an occasional nod of commiseration (*conversation*).

It has taken me much prayer and even more practice to understand the Lords direction in my life and the importance of climate control in my marriage. It is imperative that I allow the Lord freedom to change me. Only then, will I be able to change the climate of my home from the harsh cold of discord to the warmth of tender peace.

Let's look at a possible scenario that has climate control options:

Mary and John's living room is warm and inviting. It is filled soft, natural hued furniture, plush throw pillows on the couch and a fire glowing in the fireplace. John is in an oversized chair, reading his favorite book. Steam curls up from a cup of fresh coffee on the table next him. He is content, reading and resting on the first day of his weekend off.

Mary is in the kitchen, staring at the clock. It's 6:30 p.m. "Prayer meeting is in a half an hour," she sadly ponders as she stirs her cup of tea. "If John was serving God, we could go together, like other normal, married couples."

Mary placed the box of tea bags back into the cabinet and continues with her line of thinking, "Then, we could go out for coffee or a quick bite to eat with the other normal, married couples." She looked over at John and thought, "But, no. He doesn't want to go to church."

Familiar menacing words were whispered into her mind. "Your husband will never come to church. You will never fit in and you will never be of any use." It was not the first time Mary had heard them, and somehow, she knew it would not be the last time, either. Holding back hot tears, Mary stared out her kitchen window and sipped her tea in silence...

Does this scene sound or feel familiar to you? Do you think Mary's tears are hopeful or angry? What do you think her next step will be? What would yours be? Will Mary toss her cup into the sink and make a grand show of leaving for church? Or, will she give John a smooch, a little wink and a smile and tell him she's going to go to prayer meeting?

There are several ways in which this situation can be handled. All of which are dependent on the climate Mary chooses for her home. Our lives are made up of many "one scene with many options" moments. It is how we thoughtfully maneuver our way through the complexities of the situations, always considering the consequences prior to taking action. Using this type of forward thinking will help us choose the right climate for our home.

Reminders:

- It is *so much more* advantageous to be silly than stodgy.

- Hugs are better than shrugs.

- "Thank you, Honey." Goes farther than, "What? Do you want a gold star for that?!"

- "I appreciate your help" will get you a gold star before "Just get out of the way; you're causing more harm than good".

- Saying, "I am sorry" works wonders.

- Saying, "I am wrong" works miracles.

- If you say "Please" in just the right tone of voice, you can ask your husband a multiple choice question, and he will smile and answer: *D*, all of the above.

BUILDERS AND PLUCKERS

{ *Every wise woman buildeth her house:*
but the foolish plucketh it down with her hands.
Proverbs 14:1

Within every woman, there is the ability to choose whether or not to be wise or to be foolish. Wisdom uses the tools of love, good manners and respect to build a home of protection, honor and integrity. Foolishness lays its hands to the sledge hammer of anger, discontent and sorrow which demolishes a home filled with the hidden treasures of joy, happiness and hope. It is a choice that each of us has to make, everyday.

For several years, my husband was emotionally unavailable in our marriage, almost to the point of being invisible. A depression settled over me like a heavy, wet wool blanket. Each morning, it was a challenge to breathe, let alone get out of bed. I was a miserable wretch of a woman. Before I would throw off the blankets, I would whisper a desperate one-word prayer, "Jesus."

My life was consumed with running interference between my four biological children, two stepchildren, my ex-husband, his wife, my husband, his ex-wife and God. Needless to say, I was depressed, defeated and disgusted. Everywhere I turned; it felt as if I was hitting a brick wall. When I prayed, I felt defeated. When I was at church, I felt depressed. When I was at home, I was disgusted.

Anger was my closest friend and hysteria seemed like a "not so distant cousin" coming to call. I was at the end of my spiritual rope and getting ready to tie the knot onto its fraying end and hang on for dear life. I was beginning to feel like a hopeless fool of a woman wondering, "Why am I trying to make this marriage work? WHY?!"

A still small voice broke through my inner chaos and said, "Because I am in it."

"How can you be in this, Lord?"

"Because, I'm God and I'm everywhere."

Whither shall I go from thy spirit? or whither shall I flee from thy presence? If I ascend up into heaven, thou art there: if I make my bed in hell, behold, thou art there. If I take the wings of the morning, and dwell in the uttermost parts of the sea

Psalm 139:7-9

The Lord flipped on the switch of understanding, and allowed me to see the big picture. Jesus Christ is travelling this path with me to the end. Be it bitter or sweet. He let me know that I was not going to be immediately delivered *out* of my marriage, but blessed *through* it. From that day forward, I began taking baby steps to help me get my eyes off of the pain and displeasure of my marriage and focusing them on pleasing the Lord.

And if a house be divided against itself, that house cannot stand.

Mark 3:25

During this time, the state of my home was like a war-torn battle field with a line of division marked so distinctly, you felt as if you were walking through the trenches, not a kitchen. Our two sets of children played me and Rich against each other. His children complained that I wanted to know where they were at all times, and my children would complain about Rich letting their stepbrothers do "anything they wanted to do."

My children wanted to stay home from church, stay out

late, go to different worldly events, like their stepbrothers, but I stood my ground. I did not cave into the pressure and allow my children to do things I had not allowed them do prior to my marriage to Rich. It wasn't easy with one set of kids going hither and yon while mine stayed home or went to church. Believe me, I depended on the Lord, *everyday*, to help me continue standing and He has not failed me, yet!

"But ye are a chosen generation, a royal priesthood,
an holy nation, a peculiar people; that ye should shew
forth the praises of him who hath called you out of
darkness into his marvellous light;
which in time past were not a people, but are now the
people of God: which had not obtained mercy, but
now have obtained mercy."

1 Peter 2:9-10

Born again Christians are strangers in the world. When a person walks away from sin and is grafted into the household of Christ, through repentance, baptism in Jesus' name and the infilling of the Holy Ghost, they are forever changed. Regardless of their spiritual state of affairs, a Christian will never 'fit in' with the world again. Never. Ever.

Now, I felt like a stranger in my own home. I worked my family's Christianity around my husband's worldliness. In my home, I didn't have freedom to pray, worship or even listen to Christian music. There were things that I did and didn't do in order to maintain a sort of cease fire. Even though there was no physical battling going on, my family fought a vicious, never ending spiritual battle. It took every ounce of energy to stay alive.

On Sunday mornings, I dragged my battle weary bones to the house of God to be set, bandaged and healed.

Sometimes, I would sit in the pew, feeling the full heat of spiritual attack pressing me farther into my seat, as the enemy of my soul bombarded my mind with negativity and accusation:

"If you were a better wife, Rich would come to church..."

"You married him. What makes you think God will help you?"

"Give up. Just walk out. It's easier."

During the service, I could feel the pressure of condemnation closing in on me as I was crushed by an unmerciful vice of despair. My heart would break with each twist of loneliness that came from the emotional separation that was taking place between me and Rich. I felt the heaviness of every mistake I had made with my children and stepchildren. The weight of hopelessness settled on me with self-loathing as I remembered each moment of weakness, error and unwise behavior.

"Put on the whole armour of God, that ye may be able to stand against the wiles of the devil. For we wrestle not against flesh and blood, but against principalities, against powers, against the rulers of the darkness of this world, against spiritual wickedness in high places. Wherefore take unto you the whole armour of God , that ye may be able to withstand in the evil day, and having done all, to stand. Stand therefore, having your loins girt about with truth, and having on the breastplate of righteousness; And your feet shod with the preparation of the gospel of peace; Above all, taking the shield of faith, wherewith ye shall be able to quench all the fiery darts of the wicked. And take the helmet of salvation, and the sword of the Spirit, which is the word of God"

Ephesians 6:14-17

Sometimes, the battle in my mind was so intense, I had to grasp the pew in front of me with pitbull determination and *force myself* to stand in reverence to God. I called it "White Knuckle Praising" because it was a fierce struggle against my flesh. I knew if I stayed down, it would be that much longer before I was able to get up! I learned quickly that in the times when I least wanted to praise the Lord, was when it was imperative for me to praise Him the most! I knew no matter where I was, what I had done, or how I felt; Jesus Christ is God and because of that simple fact, He is worthy of any and all of my praise.

It took all the strength I could muster to perform the simple act of standing, but there I was: bloody and beaten before my King, crying, "You are the mighty God, the Alpha and Omega! I refuse to deny you the praise that already belongs to you!"

Standing represented the physical retaliation to my spiritual *attack* against the enemy! I refused to stay down and do nothing. I refused to give the enemy of my soul, *and enemy of my King*, an opportunity to gloat over my human weakness. I could not, *would not* let the Lord down! He had always been there for me and He was my only hope! And, as I stood for Jesus, strength and joy entered my spirit. I felt my sorrow and pain melt away and before I knew it, I was praising and worshipping the Lord with heartfelt abandon!

Church is the only place I have the freedom to be who and what I really am: a Christian woman. During the services, I soak up the Spirit and the Word like a hard, shriveled sponge being tossed into a bucket of warm water. I remember one service, in particular, that changed me and challenged me to acknowledge who Jesus is in my life. The text was:

> *"He saith unto them, But whom say ye that I am? And Simon*
> *Peter answered and said, Thou art the Christ, the Son of the*
> *living God. And Jesus answered and said unto him, Blessed art*
> *thou, Simon Barjona: for flesh and blood hath not revealed*

it unto thee, but my Father which is in heaven. And I say also unto thee, That thou art Peter, and upon this rock I will build my church; and the gates of hell shall not prevail against it."
Matthew 16:15-18

The Preacher asked, "Who do you say that Jesus is?" He went on to ask us if Jesus was our Christ, or had something else taken His place in our lives as Savior. I began to look at my own life and realized that compromise and cease fire had become my savior. At home, I would put Jesus in a type of holding pattern while I tip-toed around, not wanting to rock the boat. I had not placed Jesus on the throne as the Lord of all in my home, but instead had placed my husband there. During this service, the Holy Ghost led me to revelation, conviction and repentance.

"Therefore whosoever heareth these sayings of mine, and doeth them, I will liken him unto a wise man, which built his house upon a rock...and it fell not: for it was founded upon a rock. And every one that heareth these sayings of mine, and doeth them not, shall be likened unto a foolish man, which built his house upon the sand...and great was the fall of it."
Matthew 7:24-27

At that moment, the Lord gave me a vision of my home. In it, all of the floors were pits of quicksand. As I walked across them, I would get sucked under the sand until I was unable to move. This was exactly how I felt, everyday! Then, vision came to me again. This time, as I walked across the floor, a large slab of rock rose up out of the sand and met my foot with every step! The Lord spoke to my heart and told me that *I* was the church in my home: blood bought, Holy Ghost filled, established by the Word, built upon the Rock and the gates of hell would not prevail against me.

After that service, I brought home a brand new

confidence in Christ! When I stepped into my front door, the Rock met my foot. I began praying aggressively for my spiritual health and emotional well-being, so that I could effectively live for the Lord. This would enable me to be an example to my husband. When I begin to feel the heaviness of oppression sneaking over me, I take inventory of my armor. I make sure that every bit of it is intact and begin charging full speed into praising the King of Kings!

My dear sister, pay attention to your spiritual surroundings and be aware of the sneaky attacks of the enemy. Keep the armor of God on at all times! When you feel like giving up and laying down – don't do it! Grab a hold of the pew in front of you and stand at the throne of the Almighty. Be a "Pitbull of Praise" for Jesus and do an "In your face!" to the enemy.

Always remember, Jesus Christ is King; He is still on the throne and nothing will ever change that fact. So, regardless of the condition in your home, rest assured that wherever you walk, each footstep will be firmly founded on the eternal, never changing Rock, Jesus Christ.

WHEN WE WORSHIP,
WE ARE WARSHIPS!
~Christine Carney

LET GO, LET GOD
AND BE NICE

"What if He Never Gets Saved?" is a terrible question and a dreadful possibility. I know you've thought it, because I have pondered the question myself! It's possible that your husband may never serve the Lord, because, *it's his choice*. Nobody drug you to the altar by the hair and shoved the gift of the Holy Ghost down your throat! No, you did it on your own. It was your choice. And, I'm sorry ladies, but, unless your husband makes up his mind and chooses Christ for himself – no one is going to shove it down his throat, either. It is a harsh truth and it hurts, but, it is a good reason for us to grow and serve the Lord. Without nurturing spiritual growth in ourselves, we close the window of truth from which our husbands can experience the fresh, fragrant breeze of the Holy Spirit.

If years pass and you find that your man is still not saved, what happens to you if you haven't ventured out of your immediate circumstance and prospered in Christ? Do you feel as if you have wasted your entire walk with God pining away for your husband's salvation, with no growth, no fruit and no saved husband? In the end, you will have an open door and a welcome mat waiting for anger, discontent, resentment, disdain, malice, hate, bitterness and despair to come in and take up residency in your spiritual home. That is why it is of paramount importance that we ladies understand that our growth in Christ comes with being a Christian! The Savior of your soul wants to lead you into a productive and wonder filled life in Him, regardless of your situation.

During a time of trial and error with my witnessing methods attempted with Richard, I tried the old, "Tell

him that he's going to hell, but, in a joke" approach. It was funny, but, not real funny. I opened the local news paper and saw an article about micro chipping people in America. The article told about the advances in technology and how beneficial micro chipping would be for the medical community and those people with particular illnesses. I went into a mild hysteria, waving the paper and doing the "Oh Jesus!" dance in the living room.

The article told of a provider of surveillance equipment that had two of its employees implanted with glass-encapsulated microchips with miniature antennas in their forearms. The "chipping" of the two with RFID (radio frequency identification tags) was utilized to restrict access to specific areas of the company. It went onto say that over 9,000 people had been chipped already, from Alzheimer's and Diabetic patients to prisoners. It stated that the government is working on legislation that will require every baby to be chipped at birth! The article ended with a thought provoking question, 'when would the government force everyone to take the chip, or go hungry?' (Columbus Dispatch, July 22, 2007, Todd Lewan, ASSOCIATED PRESS)

Needless to say, I had an "Oh, Jesus!" moment.

Rich didn't have much to say about the matter, other than, "I won't take that thing. That'd be stupid." DUH. Then, he says something that makes me want to hit him on his head.

"It won't ever happen. People won't let the government do it."

"Rich, yes, it is going to happen. The Bible says it's going to happen. The newspaper says it's going to happen." I tell him in my quiet, oh-you're lucky I have the Holy Ghost-voice. "Maybe you'd like to think about missing that little trip to the lake of fire, babe, and serve God."

He laughed.

This is complacency, my friends, and it is why microchipping *is* going to happen. My husband's a good **guy**. **He** works, provides for his family and is kind to animals and some children. *But-*he doesn't see the sense in serving God. He does not feel it is necessary or worthwhile. Rich lives the life of complacency, and, it breaks my heart for him.

The next night, Rich tried to call me on his way home from work. I was busy with a patient and unable to get my phone, so I called him after the appointment.

He said, "Where are you? I tried to call 3-4 times!"

"I was with a client. What do you need?"

"Oh, I just got home and you weren't here and I couldn't get a hold of you..."

"And you thought the rapture really HAD taken place and you were left here on Earth to face the Antichrist and every demon of hell until the day of Judgement where you'd be thrown into the lake of fire to spend eternity wondering why you didn't go to church with me when you had a chance? How sweet, honey."

"Right. You're funny."

I recounted this particular conversation to my dear friend and "Dad" in the Lord, Robert Jones. As I chuckled at my own wit, there was silence on the other end of the line.

"Bro. Jones? Bob, are you there?"

"Yeess, Sister Chris," he said in his best you-are-going-to-get-an-earful voice. "I'm here."

"You should have heard Rich, he laughed – "

"How could you have said something as calloused as that to your husband, Sister?"

"What do you mean?" I asked, not a little shocked. "I was just being silly in a serious way."

"Chris, you know there is a chance that Rich may never become a born again Christian, right?"

"Well, yes." I said.

"And, you know where that will land him for eternity," Bro. Bob's voice was a lesson in controlled chagrin "you know the state of affairs in this world, and Rich's lack of interest in the Lord. Yet, you joke about something so serious." He continued, "Sister Chris, if your husband never chooses Christ, then, *all he has* is to be happy in this life."

I started crying, ashamed because I had yet to see things this way before.

Brother Bob heard my snorting and said, "Oh, now dry up those tears, girl, and make this life the best you can for your husband." There was a silent moment, and he added, "The memories of this life may be the only ones Rich has to take with him into eternity; make them happy ones, Chris."

"I will." I said. "Thank you."

"You are welcome."

That conversation changed my life and attitude toward Richard and my behavior regarding witnessing to him. I went home and apologized to him and told him how much I loved him. Of course, Rich just laughed and told me he knew what I meant, and that no harm was done. But, the hug he gave me afterwards told me the truth: Rich needed my apology. And, I needed his forgiveness.

This shift in the fault line of my Christian walk made me reevaluate how I represented Jesus in Richard's life. I became more and more aware of my actions toward him and around him. I became conscientious about making Jesus applicable and real in his life, instead of making it a joke or funny.

I made it my mission to make this life a happy one for my man. I wanted to be a vessel that would produce the love of Christ for Rich. It was not an easy task, but little by little, one trip to the woodshed at a time, the Lord began to teach me how to be a productive Christian and a good wife. He taught me how to be the wife that Richard needed me to be.

This is where a little disclaimer comes into play. *I can tell you* how I am becoming the wife that Rich needs me to be and things I do that make him feel special and needed.

I cannot and will not tell you how to be the wife your **husband** needs you to be. This journey is our own, my dear friend, and each woman's journey is unique from one another in every way. I will tell you this: love the Lord, love your man, pray a lot and be patient.

> *And the Lord direct your hearts into the love of God,*
>
> *and into the patient waiting for Christ.*
>
> *2 Thessalonians 3:5*

So many times, I have heard it said, and been told myself, *not* to pray for patience. I was told that if I did, the windows of heaven would open and rain fiery balls of tribulation on me. I was so afraid to pray for patience, that if by chance I spoke the words, "Lord, give me patience!" I would compulsively shout out, "NO! I take that back, in Jesus' name!"

It got to the point of being a superstitious Obsessive Compulsive Disorder, so to speak. It was ridiculous. If we need patience, then, don't you think God, being the all wise and knowing God, the one true living God, the Creator, the Alpha and Omega would know about it? And...do something about it? These are some of the things that make me go "hmmmm."

If I do not pray *for* patience, how will I ever achieve it? If I don't ask the Lord to help me with patience, who will I ask? Can a Christian have faith without patience enough to wait on the Lord for an answer? If I don't pray for patience, how will I grow and receive it? Honestly, I do not know if it is because I am getting older, but, things make more sense to me than they did when I was younger.

FREE ADVICE:
GET YOUR PATIENCE-ASSISTANCE FROM
THE LORD — HE KNOWS BEST.

A WEDDING ANNIVERSARY IS THE
CELEBRATION OF LOVE, TRUST,
PARTNERSHIP, TOLERANCE AND
TENACITY. THE ORDER VARIES
FOR ANY GIVEN YEAR.

~Paul Sweeney

COMPARISON,
CONCUPISCENCE AND
COVETOUSNESS

{ *For the unbelieving husband is sanctified by the wife...*
1 Corinthians 7:14

Perversion is the shadow of twisted lies that is cast when our flesh is placed between the light of Christ and Truth. When messages were taught using the above quoted text, I understood *sanctified* as being synonymous with the word, *saved*. This caused me great inner conflict, because, on one hand, I felt encouraged that my husband was safe, and on the other, I felt the crushing burden of responsibility for his salvation. As a result, I was keenly focused on Rich's need for salvation and my responsibility to insure it for him. By casting the shadow of salvation on sanctification, the word wife was perverted to *savior*.

In order to correct my wrong thinking, I began studying the scripture and praying for wisdom. I found reassurance and peace as the Lord led me into an understanding of His love and plan for me and my family. A simple word study set me on a course toward revelation and sanity!

Let's begin with the word, *sanctify*: it is from the Greek word *Hagiaz*, "to **acknowledge** or **render**, or to be **venerable** or **hallow**." *Sanctify* is a verb and also an adjective, it defines the action of the sanctifier and describes the one who is sanctified:

Acknowledge, n: to recognize the rights, authority, or status of, to greet, to nod

Render, n: to execute the motions of, to render a salute

Venerable, adj: (venerate) worthy of respect or reverence by reason of age and dignity, character, or position.

Hallow (to be), adj: greatly respected: venerable

The Lord regards our husbands worthy of *"respect by reason of the position"* they hold as the spouse of His daughter. With a royal nod of recognition, our Lord and King, Jesus Christ, provides our husbands extra opportunities to witness truth. It is through our steadfast service and growth in the Lord that will allow those windows of opportunity to remain open. God's favor on our husband and his salvation is dependent on our growth in God, not the other way around.

{ *But if the unbelieving depart, let him depart...*

1 Corinthians 7:15

That's about as straightforward as you can get without using a 2 x 4. Now, I will pose a question to you and I want you to really think on it. If a man is saved, or even remotely saved through marriage to a Christian woman, why would the Lord tell the wife to let him go? *Let him go.* If our duty, as wives, is to be the insurance for our husband's salvation, I believe the Lord would have worded the verse more like this, *"But if the unbelieving depart, put on your running shoes, chase him down like the dirty dog he is, and make him stay."* Maybe not exactly like that, but, you get the picture!

> *"Mortify therefore your members which are upon the earth; fornication, uncleanness, inordinate affection, evil concupiscence, and covetousness, which is idolatry: For which things' sake the wrath of God cometh on the children of disobedience: In the which ye also walked some time, when ye lived in them. But now ye also put off all these; anger, wrath, malice, blasphemy, filthy communication out of your mouth."*
> *Colossians 3:5-8*

In Lynda Allison Doty's book, *Apostolic Counseling,* she used this scripture, and expounded on verse five in a way that had a profound effect on my relationship with my husband. She wrote,

> "...mortify therefore your members which are upon the earth, fornication, uncleanness, inordinate affection, evil concupiscence and covetousness, which is idolatry...He's [God] listing these things we have to give up, we have to kill them...We cannot allow them in our lives...There are husbands, for example, who spies out another woman and like what he sees. Oh, she's got it all together. And he starts to compare her to his wife. He has got to nip that in the bud! Number one we are not to compare. And number two: you're supposed to honor your wife, you're supposed to love your wife as Christ loved the church. The wife is supposed to honor and reverence her husband." (*Apostolic Counseling,* Lynda Allison Doty, pp114-115).

Sister Doty's reference to husbands comparing their wives to other women made a direct hit into my heart and conscience. The revelation of sinful comparison came with a deep-seated conviction about my own conduct and attitudes! I was guilty of comparison.

When I began to think about it, I realized how many functions, church services and conferences I had sat through watching *all* the wives sitting there with *all* their husbands. I watched *all* the godly men worship and praise the Lord with *all* their wives. I admired their walk with God, but, I saw *everything* I did not have, and *everything* Rich was not. Sometimes, it was enough to make me cry. Other times, I just wanted to throw up!

If given the opportunity, the enemy of our souls will pervert our perceptions; twisting our thinking in order to breed discontent which will usher sin into our heart. Without an inkling of what was going on, the devil had cast the subtle shadow of discontent on Rich, and my admiration of godly men was perverted into coveting a *type* of man that my husband was not. When we attach a face to the spiritual assets we desire for our husbands, it becomes sin. I could not believe I had fallen for that trick! I did not realize what I was doing!

Longing for your husband to experience the wonderful spiritual gifts that the Lord has available to him is not a sin. Neither is the desire to see your husband worshipping and praising the Lord at your side. But, when we look at a man-*any man*-and yearn for our husband to behave the way that particular man does, it becomes sin. And, we must put it under the blood-*pronto*- and move on!

> *...evil concupiscence, and*
> *covetousness, which is idolatry.*
> *For which things' sake the wrath of God*
> *cometh on the children of disobedience*
> *Colossians 3:5*

Concupiscence is the Greek word **epithymia.**

Epithymia, desire, craving, longing, desire for what is forbidden.

Epi, to be on top of, upon, over, before, dominant.

Thymia, indicating a certain emotional condition, mood, or state of mind.

When our thoughts are dominated with a desire of things forbidden to us, *or things we do not possess*, it is concupiscence. In my case, I became fixated on the fact that *I didn't have a Christian husband,* my husband's faults, and the *traits of a Christian that he did not possess.* I then began comparing my husband's lack of spirituality to Christian men who had an abundant supply. If you have the thought that starts with something like, 'Look at Bro. So-n-So...I wish...' recognize it as a spiritual attack and an attempt to pervert your admiration into condemnation. Regardless of how innocent the intent of your heart, consider these thoughts as sin and cast them back into the halls of darkness where they came from!

If these thoughts are not dealt with quickly, they will become covetous. The Greek word for covetousness is *pleonexia*, which means to have the insatiable desire to have what rightfully belongs to others. *Pleonexia* is a Greek philosophical concept inculcated in the writings of Plato and Aristotle. It is the harsh desire to have more, specifically, the yearning after money and power. Those who are covetous "act like the world revolves around them."

Pleonexia, callous, egotistical and pompous assumption that others and things exist to be used solely for one's own purpose.

Pleo, excessive desire

Nex, murder, violence

Covetousness is the state of mind that ignores the needs of others and focuses solely on their personal lusts and desires; justifying their sin, even when it causes the violent death of their marriage, family and relationship with God.

> But every man is tempted, when he is drawn away
> of his own lust, and enticed. Then when lust hath
> conceived, it bringeth forth sin: and sin,
> when it is finished, bringeth forth death.
> *James 1:14–15*

We are absolutely **not** to compare our own dear (and, not so dear) husbands with those men who belong to other women! It is idolatry and we must protect our thoughts from being dominated by the type of husband we do not have and the faults of the husband we do have. This type of thinking leaves the door wide open for discontentment, and if left unchecked, it will *bring forth* concupiscence and covetousness. If we still refuse to bring these thoughts under submission to the Lord, it will become the sin of *mind-full* fornication. This can sever the emotional tethers God has placed on us to our husbands. Then, our sin will *bring forth* spiritual and marital death.

> *To whom ye forgive any thing, I forgive also: for if I forgave any thing, to whom I forgave it, for your sakes forgave I it in the person of Christ; Lest Satan should get an advantage of us: for we are not ignorant of his devices.*
>
> 2 Corinthians 20:11

We must know the deceitful devices of the devil and crush them before they take root in our marriage! It is our duty to rise above the situation within our home, bring down the stronghold of sin, and soar into the heights the Lord has for us! Let us grow together and become a catalyst for revival, instead of being stuck in the miry mess of sin and discontent!

Flourish in God and seek his will for your life. The Lord favors our husbands with extra *opportunities* to experience truth through our marriage. However, there are countless other people who will meet Christ only once in their life time, and that chance meeting could very well be with you. This is why it is of paramount importance for us to grow and prosper in the things of the Lord.

If we remain stagnant and unchanged in our walk with God, what good reason have we given our husbands to entertain the idea of Christianity? What proof can we offer? What motivation do they have to lay down their current lifestyle and choose Christ? You cannot convince anyone that serving the Lord it is worth pursuing, if they do not see any evidence to convince them otherwise. The

Lord will provide our husband the physical proof of his existence through our consistent and heartfelt growth as Christians.

Trying to reach our husbands without growing and maturing as a Christian, is like trying to sell him a shriveled up bulb, a pack of tiny seeds, some horse manure and a shovel with the promise of a beautiful garden filled with lush, fragrant flowers. How do you convince a person who has never experienced the explosive beauty of a garden in full, kaleidoscopic bloom that it came from these ugly dried up seeds and bulbs? Who would blame them for declining the offer of hard, stinky work with no visible profit?

It is the vibrant growth in our everyday life that makes Christ a reality in our husband's life. If we don't grow into the brilliant blossom that the Lord intends for us to be, we will never win our husbands (or anyone!) to Christ.

By their marriage to the King's daughters, these men of ours are sanctified; recognized and acknowledged for their position as our husband. Because of this, the King will allow him special opportunities to find Truth through us, His beloved daughters. But, our husband's salvation is solely dependent on *his* choice to repent, to be baptized in Jesus' name and receive the promise of the Holy Ghost— just like you and I did.

To keep your marriage brimming,
With love in the loving cup,
Whenever you're wrong, admit it;
Whenever you're right, shut up.
~Ogden Nash

MARRIAGE CERTIFICATE
OF EXPERIENCE

IF YOU CAN LOOK INTO THE SEEDS
OF TIME, AND SAY WHICH GRAIN
WILL GROW AND WHICH WILL NOT,
SPEAK THEN TO ME.
~William Shakespeare

This chapter is *all about you* and why being married offers us a Certificate of Experience. It is in God's plan to use you in any capacity He chooses, if you are willing to be used. In the next few pages, we will discuss the benefits of simply being married, period. A married woman is perceived by the general population as more stable, established and dependable than our single counterparts. Prejudice? Perhaps. But, that's the way it is.

Insurance companies and employers perceive married women as more stable and responsible. If you're over forty-even better! In 1985, Bradley University performed a study to determine a whether or not society had a perceptual bias on women, based on employment and marital status. The group found the personality traits of married women *were perceived* more positively than those of unmarried women. I say take advantage of that one, ladies, because we can hide some of our quirky personality flaws, that if we were single, regardless of age, we would not be able to!

*"The aged women likewise, that they be in behaviour as
becometh holiness, not false accusers, not given to much wine,
teachers of good things; That they may teach the young women
to be sober, to love their husbands, to love their children, To be
discreet, chaste, keepers at home, good, obedient to their own
husbands, that the word of God be not blasphemed."*
Titus 2:3-5

Unfortunately, the Lord's natural order and plan for
his daughters has been skewed by social changes, feminism
and sin. Women have become inordinately competitive
with each other, and have replaced the Biblical benefits
of female relationships with the fear and apprehension of
an enemy. By being married, the perceived "threat" level
decreases and acceptance increases among the ranks of
womankind.

A few years ago, I went to Amish country with my
friend, Kathy and pulled into the parking lot of a local
grocery store. As we walked toward the entrance, we passed
a young, very-pregnant Amish woman with six children in
tow. A store clerk followed the family, pulling a cart of ten
bushels of apples to her buggy. It was obvious the apples
were not going to fit into the buggy and she was going to
need some sort of assistance. Kathy and I watched the
young woman, looked at each other and turned around in
silent agreement.

We approached her buggy and introduced ourselves.
Then, we asked the young woman, Mary, if she'd like help
loading the apples into her buggy and what apples would
not fit, we would carry in our Jeep to her home. After some
pleasant and cordial declines, Mary said, with a distinctive
German accent, "If you do not mind, it will help me
immensely. But, I go slow, and it is a little bit far." Kathy
and I laughed and assured her there was nothing we would
rather do!

Driving between ten and fifteen miles per hour, we

followed the black buggy as it clop-clop-clopped along the winding country roads. The rolling hills were quilted with the luscious colors of fall. When we arrived at our destination, it was not one of the wealthy, picturesque Amish homesteads portrayed in paintings, brochures and book covers. But, it was a large, sprawling farm with a few horses and cows hanging around the field, a couple of sorry looking pigs in a pen and a dozen or so scrawny chickens littering the yard. This was real life Amish: hard work, low pay, lots of kids and no lights.

As we drove up the gravel drive way, Mary's husband was bringing the draught horses into the barn. When the buggy approached the barn, he took the reins of the horse and brought the buggy to a complete stop.

After we unloaded the apples, Kathy and I had an interesting conversation with Mary and her husband, John. Mary confided that she'd been having some trouble with her pregnancy and I began to offer some advice. Before I got the first sentence out, Mary looked me square in the eye and asked, "Are you married?" I told her that I was; then she asked with a firm tone, "Then, how old are you?" Taken aback, I sputtered and joked, "Oh, this is my third or fourth year being thirty nine!"

Mary looked at me and laughed, "You English women are so strange. We do not understand why you are so concerned about age. For us, we need to know how old a woman is before we listen to what they say." She continued, "If you are my age, then you do not know much more than I do, but, if you are older and if you are married, I will listen."

Amish women consider older, married or widowed women wiser and more trustworthy. The married woman will not consider a younger or single woman's opinion, view, or advice over that of a more seasoned woman. The Amish place a high value on age, experience and marital status when seeking counsel.

Sister, you and I are part of an elite group of highly skilled and experienced women who are called by the Most High to fulfill an urgent need in His kingdom. Our marital status, alone, offers us a broader base of women with whom we can reach: single, newly married, middle married or "rock solid in the zone" married. Our testimony is fuller, more colorful, spotted with faith building trials, and encouraging victories softened with tears and molded by the hands of the mighty Potter, Himself. The diversity of our experiences enables us to reach all women and teach most. We have skills and the Lord wants us to be *available* to use them!

God has used many women who were married to men that did not serve Him: a prophetess and judge, a mom of a pastor and a woman who became Queen. In the following chapters, we are going to look at the lives of Deborah, Eunice and Abigail. These women refused to be hindered by their husband's lack of service and lack of obedience to God. They forged ahead into His plan and left an example of tremendous victory and fruitfulness for us to learn from and model our lives by. The Lord desires to use all of us, but, He will use only those who are *willing to be used*.

I AM STILL DETERMINED TO BE
CHEERFUL AND HAPPY, IN WHATEVER
SITUATION I MAY BE; FOR I HAVE ALSO
LEARNED FROM EXPERIENCE THAT
THE GREATER PART OF OUR HAPPINESS
OR MISERY DEPENDS UPON OUR
DISPOSITIONS, AND NOT UPON OUR
CIRCUMSTANCES.
~Martha Washington

THE TALE OF FOUR LADIES: THREE WHO DID AND ONE WHO DID NOT

Many women who are married to unsaved spouses tend to believe their husbands' salvation is the crux of their walk with God and any possible ministry in their life. The Bible contradicts this view with Deborah, Abigail and Eunice and admonishes us with Naomi...

Deborah

I believe one of the greatest role models for today's woman is Deborah. She is strong, gutsy and doesn't put up with much *stuff*. I am intrigued by her spunk and dedication to God and His people, even though her husband did not serve the Lord. Many women feel inadequate for a leadership role in the church because of their unevenly yoked marriage.

Take heart, dear Sister! Look at Deborah!

She was a prophetess, a title no other judge possessed.

She was a judge; a title no other woman possessed.

Deborah was not just any prophet, but she was a prophet during the time of war...

> *And Deborah, a prophetess, the wife of*
> *Lapidoth, she judged Israel at that time.*
> *Judges 4:4*

Lapidoth is introduced to us for no other reason than to identify his wife. The Bible mentions him only one time, and that as part of our introduction to the prophetess and judge, Deborah. Lapidoth: One man, one introduction, no further elucidation other than to identify a woman's marital status.

According to Jewish custom, at the time of marriage, the husband is to give his future wife a *ketubah*. This is a marriage document which specifies the physical and emotional responsibilities of the husband to his wife, as well as, his financial obligations in the case of divorce. It's an ancient pre-nuptial contract created to protect women from being kicked to the curb by their husbands, with no help or hope of an income. This liberated the wife by guaranteeing her with physical and financial stability. Deborah's *ketubah* allowed her respect, income and the status needed to respond to the needs of a nation with quick decisive action.

The name, Lapidoth, gives us insight into his spiritual relationship with God and his wife, Deborah.

Lapidoth is from the Hebrew word, Lappiyd:

1. A torch 'despised'
2. Cast aside, because of its' having ceased to give light
3. An image for a man formerly highly esteemed, but now low and despised

I purport that Lapidoth was called to do great things for the Lord, but, stopped short, gave up and backslid. His name suggests that he held and lost an estimable position, leaving him despised by the people and cast aside by the Lord. The fact that Lapidoth is never mentioned again leads me to believe that he was uninvolved and uninterested with Deborah's spiritual life. The one notable thing he did was to marry Deborah; therefore, giving her the status, respectability and freedom to fulfill God's calling in her life.

With Lapidoth content to be in the background, Deborah was able to get up and go when certain situations presented themselves. Had Lapidoth been a tyrant or any other man, Deborah would have perhaps had more of a struggle in her service to the Lord.

In the same manner, Deborah's name reveals much about her character:

Deborah is from the Hebrew, Debowrah:

1. Bee, swarm
2. Orderly, unity

Debowrah is from the root word, debar:

1. To speak, declare, converse
2. To speak with one another
3. To command, promise, warn, threaten
4. Lead away, put to flight
5. Sing

You might be wondering about Deborah's name meaning "bee, swarm, orderly and unity" all at the same time. It makes me want to start singing that old Sesame Street song, "One of these things do not belong here...!" Not so. Bees swarm in an orderly fashion under the leadership of one queen bee.

WHAT IS NOT GOOD FOR THE SWARM IS NOT GOOD FOR THE BEE.
~Marcus Aurelius

A queen bee will command a swarm only when the survival of the hive is at risk or if the current hive is overpopulated. There are days of preparation and planning before the bees will swarm to their new living arrangement. New eggs are laid, drones fill up with honey and scout bees are sent out in search of an appropriate hive location. Only then, when all preparation is complete, does the queen lead the band of bees, in unison and en masse, to their new abode.

> *And she dwelt under the palm tree of Deborah between Ramah and Bethel in mount Ephraim: and the children of Israel came up to her for judgment.*
> *Judges 4:5*

This scripture reveals that Deborah spent her days away from her home, which allows us to deduce that she had already reared her children and settled into another phase of her life. I can almost hear Deborah say, "Empty nest, schmempty-nest! What can I do for the Lord?!" Her life remained focused on the Lord and Deborah served the Almighty God with robust zeal and dedication.

> The inhabitants of the villages ceased, they ceased in Israel,
> until that I Deborah arose, that I arose a mother in Israel.
> Judges 5:7

Deborah was also a *woman of a certain age*, because, according to the Scripture, she had been around long enough to watch the people leave the villages and see the nation's leadership decay. The Lord called Deborah to arise as a mother in Israel and she responded! The people recognized Deborah as one who possessed wisdom and came to her for sound judgment and counsel that guided the erring nation of Israel back toward faithful obedience.

You and I have come to a time in our lives where God is calling us to a place that *only we can fill*. If you are like me, and your children are grown and out of the house, then, take a moment to listen to the voice of God calling you into Him. The ministry God has chosen for us is about to be opened right before our eyes! So, let's get our eyes off of our current earthly situation and place them on our eternal and heavenly obligation.

> *"And she sent and called Barak the son of Abinoam out of*
> *Kedeshnaphtali, and said unto him, Hath not the LORD God of*
> *Israel commanded, saying, Go and draw toward mount Tabor,*
> *and take with thee ten thousand men of the children of Naphtali*
> *and of the children of Zebulun? And I will draw unto thee to the*
> *river Kishon Sisera, the captain of Jabin's army, with his chariots*
> *and his multitude; and I will deliver him into thine hand. And*
> *Barak said unto her, If thou wilt go with me, then I will go: but if*
> *thou wilt not go with me, then I will not go. And she said, I will*
> *surely go with thee: notwithstanding the journey that thou takest*
> *shall not be for thine honour; for the LORD shall sell Sisera into*
> *the hand of a woman. And Deborah arose, and went with Barak*
> *to Kedesh. And Barak called Zebulun and Naphtali to Kedesh;*
> *and he went up with ten thousand men at his feet: and Deborah*

went up with him. Now Heber the Kenite, which was of the children of Hobab the father in law of Moses, had severed himself from the Kenites, and pitched his tent unto the plain of Zaanaim, which is by Kedesh. And they shewed Sisera that Barak the son of Abinoam was gone up to mount Tabor. And Sisera gathered together all his chariots, even nine hundred chariots of iron, and all the people that were with him, from Harosheth of the Gentiles unto the river of Kishon. And Deborah said unto Barak, Up; for this is the day in which the LORD hath delivered Sisera into thine hand: is not the LORD gone out before thee? So Barak went down from mount Tabor, and ten thousand men after him."
Judges 4:6-14

God called the woman Deborah, wife of Lapidoth, to be a prophetess and war judge for the people of Israel. I have often heard it said that God only used a woman (I know what you're thinking, but, that's not where I'm going), because there was no man available. Now, I find it very difficult to believe that the Almighty God could not "find" one, single, solitary man capable of doing the job in twenty years time, particularly when Barak was right there. The Lord had placed a specific calling on Deborah's life that she, alone, had the ability to fulfill.

Deborah is a superlative example of how *God can, and will, use* a woman married to an invisible man. She stayed faithful, dedicated and *responded* when called upon by the Lord! There are things that only we can do, people only we can reach and prayers only we know how to pray! Deborah's legacy charges us to put our shoulder to shield, hand to sword, fight the battle, win the war and restore a people!

God is calling you to arms; how will you respond?

Abigail

"And there was a man in Maon, whose possessions were in

Carmel; and the man was very great, and he had three thousand

sheep, and a thousand goats: and he was shearing his sheep in

Carmel. Now the name of the man was Nabal; and the name of

his wife Abigail: and she was a woman of good understanding,

and of a beautiful countenance: but the man was churlish and

evil in his doings; and he was of the house of Caleb."

1 Samuel 25:2-3

Abigail married Prince Charming and woke up with The Beast. If you are a woman who married the handsome, charming and gainfully employed Prince of your dreams and woke up the day after your wedding to a different man; this chapter is for you. I do not believe, for one moment, that Abigail married Nabal knowing the nature of man he was. Nor do I believe Abigail's father would have contracted this marriage had Nabal revealed his true self prior to the betrothal. I encourage you to cling to Abigail and her example of a godly woman who married one man and ended up with another!

According to Jewish custom, the father would arrange the match and contract a marriage for his son or daughter. It was a two-part contract, consisting of a betrothal and an actual marriage ceremony. The betrothal was typically done when the children were young. This was a legally binding marriage contract. So much so, that in order to released from it, a letter of divorce had to be written and any penalties paid. When the children became old enough to live together as man and wife, the marriage ceremony was performed, and with a great procession, the young bride was taken from her father's home to that of her husband. And, they lived happily ever after. Or, not.

In those days, marriage was more of a business transaction than a matter of the heart, or *l'amore*. The father of the groom had to pay the bride's father a dowry that involved an exchange of money, land, animals or services. The father of the bride made no payment, knowing that there was nothing that could add to the value of his daughter. The father's choice of wife for his son was far more important than a business affair; *it was an investment*.

Nabal's father knew his churlish son, and must have been a shrewd and generous business man to convince Abigail's father to allow her to marry him. Money was no object. So, Nabal's father brought gold, land, livestock, a home, possessions, and the *house of Caleb* pedigree to the table for Abigail's hand in marriage. He knew real value when he saw it, and Abigail was a rare gem of a girl who was worth any price!

Abigail's name gives us a clear idea of her position in her father's heart. Her name is the Hebrew word, *'Abiygayil,* a combination of two words, *'ab* and *giyl*. Literally translated, Abigail's name means "my father rejoices" or in more modern terminology, "Daddy's Girl." With a name like that, you better believe Abigail would *never* be given in marriage to just anyone!

Abigail's father may or may not have known the true nature of Nabal, but the fact remains that a marriage proposal was placed on the table and he was considering it. However, I do not believe for one moment, that he would sign over his 'baby girl' without first consulting her. It makes sense that Abigail would have a choice in whom she married and that her heart's desire would sway her father's final decision.

Abigail and Nabal may have already fallen head over heels in love with each other. Nabal could have charmed Abigail with flowers, love notes and stolen kisses. Abigail may have swooned at the sight of Nabal's broad shoulders, or got lost in his smoldering dark eyes. There may have been nothing Abigail's father could say or do to change his little girls mind.

Either way, Abigail said, "I'll take him!"

The "I do's" were spoken, the honeymoon was taken and the coffee started brewing.

Good Morning, Sunshine! Welcome to the real life of a woman married to a complete idiot. Abigail's idyllic dreams of being the 'perfect couple' were shattered. Her charming cavalier who wooed and romanced her was gone, and Abigail found out soon enough that he was the epitome of his name. *Nabal* is the word used throughout Scripture for fool, abandoned, senseless and ungodly.

> The fool [nabal] hath said in his heart,
> There is no God. They are corrupt, they have done
> abominable works, there is none that doeth good.
> Psalm 14:1 [brackets mine]

Have you ever stood up too fast, begin to black out and see stars? Do you remember the sickening nausea rolling through your body, making your head swim until you sat down and put your head between your knees? Well, imagine all of that, only without the relief and you have a vague idea of how Abigail must have felt when she realized the true nature of her husband.

There isn't enough romance in the world that can make up for being married to a man whose name tag says, "Hello there, my name is Moron."

> ...she was a woman of good understanding, and of a
> beautiful countenance...
> 1 Samuel 25:3

Strong's Concordance describes Abigail as a person who was morally good, prudent, and with excellent insight and intuition. She had the business savvy to run a prosperous household. Abigail didn't acquire these attributes over night. They were established through time, experience and by the grace of God.

> A capable, intelligent, and virtuous woman — who is he who can find her? She is far more precious than jewels and her value is far above rubies or pearls.
> Proverbs 31:10 (AMP)

Abigail was locked into a marriage with Nabal, and it was what it was. She kept her wits about her and maintained her faith in God. She did not sit around pouting, but instead became a pillar of strength and stability for her household, staff and community. The Lord establishes Abigail's authority in the following scripture:

> "But one of the young men told Abigail, Nabal's wife, saying, Behold, David sent messengers out of the wilderness to salute our master; and he railed on them. But the men were very good unto us, and we were not hurt, neither missed we any thing, as long as we were conversant with them, when we were in the fields: They were a wall unto us both by night and day, all the while we were with them keeping the sheep. Now therefore know and consider what thou wilt do; for evil is determined against our master, and against all his household: for he is such a son of Belial, that a man cannot speak to him."
> 1 Samuel 25:14-17

The young man comes to Abigail for a solution, with confident expectation of her action. She does not correct him or send him to a manager of the estate. No. Abigail takes decisive action and gives the servant instructions.

"Then Abigail made haste, and took two hundred loaves, and two bottles of wine, and five sheep ready dressed, and five measures of parched corn, and an hundred clusters of raisins, and two hundred cakes of figs, and laid them on asses. And she said unto her servants, Go on before me; behold, I come after you. But she told not her husband Nabal. And it was so, as she rode on the ass, that she came down by the covert on the hill, and, behold, David and his men came down against her; and she met them."

1 Samuel 25:18-20

There will be times in our lives when it's prudent to remain quiet and meet the Lord "by the covert on the hill." My favorite covert is the shower. Some of my best prayer meetings have been underwater! Another place where I enjoy meeting the Lord is in my van while I'm driving to work. As long as I maintain contact with the King, I will grow and prosper in my spiritual walk with Christ. The sacrifice I make in private, the Lord will bless in the open.

But when thou doest alms, let not thy left hand know what thy right hand doeth: That thine alms may be in secret: and thy Father which seeth in secret himself shall reward thee openly.
Matthew 6:3-4

Abigail served God in the midst of a terrible marriage to a man filled with anger and rage. Scripture never states that Nabal ever raised a hand to his wife, but it does say that he was violent. The initiative Abigail took within her home demonstrates a certain amount of freedom and liberty. Her status as Nabal's wife enabled her to protect their household, belongings and land from certain destruction by David.

The Lord blessed Abigail's faithful service by allowing

her to find favor in the eyes of David, the future king of Israel. David so admired her wisdom, honest humility and graceful behavior that he blessed her in front of all his men and those of Nabal.

"And David said to Abigail, Blessed be the LORD God of Israel,

which sent thee this day to meet me: And blessed be thy advice,

and blessed be thou, which hast kept me this day from coming

to shed blood, and from avenging myself with mine own hand...

So David received of her hand that which she had brought him,

and said unto her, Go up in peace to thine house; see, I have

hearkened to thy voice, and have accepted thy person."

1 Samuel 25:32-33, 35

God honored our dear Abigail. Was it easy? No. Was it a short term walk for Abigail? No. Did she stick with the program and stay faithful? Yes, and through intercession with the Lord and humble service, she obtained the salvation of the people who lived under her roof. Abigail would never been able to do those things had she not been married to a churlish, fool of man who could not see the jewel he had in life, in a home, and especially in a wife.

Look at the example Abigail gives us of a woman married to an unsaved man. She admonishes us to remain strong, to grow, to flourish and serve the King! The Lord blessed her with a ministry that is still working and altering lives. Go to Abigail as a friend, gleaning wisdom and advice from her story.

She's available every day for counsel in 1 Samuel, chapter 25.

Eunice

> *Then came he to Derbe and Lystra: and, behold, a certain disciple*
> *was there, named Timotheus, the son of a certain woman, which*
> *was a Jewess, and believed; but his father was a Greek.*
>
> *Acts 16:1*

Eunice's story is not simply about the marriage of a Christian woman to a non-Christian man. It is one woman's proclamation of love and dedication for her God, her husband and family in the face of many obstacles. The Scripture declares her faithful service, unyielding faith and consistent growth in Christ that kept her family intact and prosperous.

The Bible introduces Eunice as a Jewess *and a believer*. Her husband is simply introduced as a Greek, *without the mention of a name*, and from henceforth, will be known as, "The Greek." The blunt exclusion of a name clearly delineates the spiritual condition and religious beliefs of Eunice to that of her husband.

Let's take a quick look at the differences, shall we?

Jewess, means that Eunice belonged to and was identified by the Jewish nation. *Judaism is monotheistic* and considers the concept of multiple gods (polytheism) heretical. The prayer, *Shema Yisrael* (Deuteronomy 6:4), perfectly encapsulates the oneness of God: "Hear, O Israel: The LORD our God is one LORD."

In Acts 16:1, *believed* is contrived of two words: *pistos*, an adjective and *peith*, a verb. It is one word that describes a person who is convinced (*pistos*) that Jesus is the Messiah and obeys (*peitho*) the gospel. The book of Acts is a clear and concise depiction of those people who *believed*. In chapter two, the crowd is convinced and accepts (*pistos*) that Christ was the Messiah. Immediately, they desire to know how to obey and comply (*peitho*) with the gospel. In response, verse 38 states, "Then Peter said unto them, Repent, and be baptized every one of you in the name of Jesus Christ for the remission of sins, and ye shall receive the gift of the Holy Ghost." In order to become a Christian, Eunice had to first believe.

Scripture states that Eunice was married to a *Greek*, which is translated to the word, *Hellen*. Strong's Concordance states that *Hellen* "embraces all nations not Jews that made the language, customs, and learning of the Greeks their own; the primary reference is to a difference of religion and worship." The word, *Greece*, means "miry or unstable one" which might indicate the type of personality Eunice's husband might possess. (A great guy who is an emotional vacuum with a shorted out cord comes to my mind...how about you?)

The *Hellenistic religion* is polytheistic, embracing many gods. It consists of *many* different philosophies, superstitions, including mysticism and astrology. Plainly stated, the Greeks were known to believe that *whatever a man or woman thought to be God*, was indeed, God.

The Bible gives us the perfect description of the Greek people:

"Then certain philosophers of the Epicureans, and of the Stoicks, encountered him. And some said, What will this babbler say? other some, He seemeth to be a setter forth of strange gods: because he preached unto them Jesus, and the resurrection. And they took him, and brought him unto Areopagus, saying, May we know what this new doctrine, whereof thou speakest, is? For thou bringest certain strange things to our ears: we would know therefore what these things mean. (For all the Athenians and strangers which were there spent their time in nothing else, but either to tell, or to hear some new thing.)

Then Paul stood in the midst of Mars' hill, and said, Ye men of

Athens, I perceive that in all things ye are too superstitious.

For as I passed by, and beheld your devotions, I found an altar

with this inscription, TO THE UNKNOWN GOD. Whom

therefore ye ignorantly worship, him declare I unto you."

Acts 17:18-23

Having a husband and son are two things that are difficult on a good day. However, Eunice had a successful marriage and she raised her only son, Timothy, to be a Preacher of the Gospel *while being married to an unsaved and unnamed man!* She is a testament to women today, of how *one woman's* faith, growth and service to God can produce world-changing results.

Like Eunice, I am a missionary in my own home and the spiritual battle never stops and the enemy never takes a break. From the moment I set my feet to the floor in the morning and throughout the day, I am in a battle against worldliness: bad language, inappropriate television shows and movies, evil beliefs and practices. Every day, I have the opportunity to show my family the reality of Jesus Christ, and my children, whether at home and grown, are watching me. Eunice trained Timothy to serve Jesus Christ while fighting the same enemy we fight, today.

When I call to remembrance the unfeigned faith that is in

thee, which dwelt first in thy grandmother Lois, and thy

mother Eunice; and I am persuaded that in thee also.

2 Timothy 1:5

Timothy's upbringing and salvation were entirely dependent on Eunice, her faith, convictions and her consistent walk with God. Where would Timothy have ended up, if Eunice had focused all her efforts on the

Greek's salvation? What if she had become discouraged and decided it was easier to follow her husband's beliefs than to convince him of her own? I'll tell you what: we may have ended up with the books of First and Second Haroldius, because God will raise up *someone who will* serve Him.

As a parent, Eunice may have been *alone spiritually* in her home, but, she was far from being *spiritually alone*. We have a mighty God to call on for help and He is able to do all things very well! Although we face very difficult situations, we can have the confidence that Jesus has already visited this moment long before we got there and is able to handle it. Eunice was a wonderful woman who heeded the call of God in her life. Today, we can learn from her direction and fulfill the ministry the Lord sets before us: Motherhood, Shepherdess, Spiritual Leader and Example of Service.

My own experience in this area is with my own son, Micaiah. He is *my* youngest child and when he turned sixteen, he desperately wanted to get his driver's license. My husband, Rich was not keen on the idea of Micaiah driving. And, Micaiah wasn't keen on the idea of *not driving*. Each of them hunted me down to bend my ear with arguments of "why he shouldn't" and "why I should." I wanted to run and hide, but instead, I ran interference, spending all my time and energy trying to please *both of them*, keep the peace and *make everybody happy*. I felt like the only ball at a ping-pong championship!

Richard's biggest complaint about Micaiah getting his license was about money and the cost of insurance. Micaiah's insurance rates would be high, but they would be even higher if he did not take driver's education. The cost of the driver's education class was over three hundred dollars and the insurance would cost one hundred dollars per month. Rich adamantly stood his ground and there was *no way* we were going to pay for it. The challenge was set before us: Micaiah pays for driver's education and insurance, Micaiah drives.

> The words of king Lemuel, the prophecy that his mother
> taught him. What, my son? and what, the son of my
> womb? and what, the son of my vows?
>
> Proverbs 31:1-2

This Scripture imparts to us the importance of a mother's godly teaching and example in a child's life. If King Lemuel heeded his mother's advice, who am I to shirk my responsibility to my own son?

I needed wisdom before I could lead Micaiah, so I went to the Lord in prayer:

Lord, you see my situation and my desire to maintain peace in my family and bring honor to You. I need your help. I need you to be Micaiah's Dad. I do not know how to handle this whole driver's education and Richard thing, and I don't want to rock the boat. But, I want Micaiah to enjoy his last years of high school and I know he wants his license. Lord, you are his Dad, you say in your word that you will be a Father to the fatherless. I need you now, Lord. Please, allow Micaiah to take Driver's Ed and get his driver's license. I'm at a loss and I do not know what to do. Thank you for listening. Thank you for handling this, Lord. I love you.

The Lord met me at that prayer altar and gave me direction on I was to handle this situation. First, I was to speak to Rich and make sure I was completely clear on the requirements for Micaiah to get his driver's license. Second, I was to explain *our* conditions to Micaiah and instruct him to go to the Lord in prayer for this need. That was it. My job was done.

One day after school, Micaiah asked if I minded him volunteering for a charity event at school that night. At first, I said no, it was a school night and he had homework and chores to do. But, at the end of my reasons, there was a nudging in my spirit and I said "no problem."

Around ten o'clock, I got a call from Micaiah.

"Hey, Mom!"

"Yes."

"I *need* to take Driver's Ed, Mom." Micaiah said with a very insistent tone.

"Micaiah, did you have to call me just to say that?" I sighed.

"No, I mean it! *Now* I *have* to take Driver's Ed!" He said with determination.

"What exactly do you mean by *you have to take it, now?*" I asked with as much patience as possible.

"Because, Mom, I won free Driver's ED classes at the charity!" Micaiah did a war-whoop and said, "God is so good, Mom! Praise you, Jesus!"

After a few minutes of doing the cell phone happy dance, I heard him say, "Mom, I gotta go! I love you, and thanks for praying for me!"

Micaiah and I recall that day often and praise the Lord for his kindness and love toward us. Only the Lord could have taken such complete care of our precarious situation, with peace, kindness and to *everyone's* satisfaction. It was a faith building milestone in Micaiah's life and only one of the many instances the Almighty God has stepped in and become his Dad!

My focus and service must be to God first, and then, He puts the rest of my life in order. I am to be an example and a faithful servant to God in order for Micaiah to learn how to be the same. It is the wisdom of the Lord that I depend on for direction in my life as a Christian wife, mom, and step mom.

If I will not grow and answer the call of God, I will not reach or teach those that live with me. The Lord can use me, because of my marriage to Rich. In this particular incidence, had I not been married, this precious lesson of faith would not have happened. My son would have missed out on a great testimony!

Rest assured, the enemy knows the power of a praying woman, but when she's a Mama, the stakes are higher, the battles more furious and the consequences **infinite**! The choices that we, as mothers, make today will affect generations of people, for good or for bad. Our children need a Godly example in their lives, and when they are growing up in a spiritually divided household, we are it. The ministry of motherhood is one that reaches far beyond our children, into the future.

I find it interesting that Eunice's name means "to fare well, live victorious," because it is a blend of attributes that Abigail and Deborah both possessed. To *"fare well"* is to be successful or do well, just as the Scripture described Abigail's ability to take charge of a household and successfully serve a king. To *"live victorious"* represents the lessons she learned from Deborah, who courageously faced the battle set before her and won.

Deborah changed the course of a nation. Abigail saved her household and all that she had from annihilation. Eunice had a successful marriage and reared her son to be a Pastor. These women lived spirit filled, productive, and victorious lives while married to unsaved men. We must embrace the legacy passed down to us by our predecessors and learn how to look beyond our circumstances to a wonderful life in God that is waiting for us!

ALMIGHTY GOD HAS GIVEN US A
RICH HISTORY — LET'S USE IT AS
A GUIDE FOR OUR PRESENT, AND
A HOPE FOR OUR FUTURE!

Naomi

WHATSOEVER WE HAVE OVER-LOVED,
IDOLIZED, AND LEANED UPON, GOD
HAS FROM TIME TO TIME BROKEN IT,
AND MADE US TO SEE THE VANITY OF
IT; SO THAT WE FIND THE READIEST
COURSE TO BE RID OUR COMFORTS IS
TO SET OUR HEARTS INORDINATELY OR
IMMODERATELY UPON THEM.

~John Flavel

If you are *in love* with a wonderful guy who has you wrapped around his little finger, and you are *"a girl who can't say no"* — this chapter is for you. Naomi felt the same way about her husband, and ended up following him into spiritual dry places. In the next few pages, we will learn about Naomi and the *ugly truth* of love, betrayal and redemption. But, we must start at the beginning in order to understand the end.

"Now it came to pass in the days when the judges ruled,
that there was a famine in the land. And a certain
man of Bethlehemjudah went to sojourn in the country
of Moab, he, and his wife, and his two sons. And the
name of the man was Elimelech, and the name of his
wife Naomi, and the name of his two sons Mahlon and
Chilion, Ephrathites of Bethlehemjudah. And they came
into the country of Moab, and continued there."

Ruth 1:1-2

Elimelech and Naomi dwelled in the land God had set aside for his people, *Bethlehemjudah*, which means *the house of bread, praise and thanksgiving.* The protection of God, the Word, and the Law surrounded those who resided in the city. The scripture states that Elimelech and his family were *Ephrathites*, natives of Ephrath, another name for Bethlehem, and had lived their whole lives in the area. Most likely, they were born and raised among God's separated people and possessed a foundation of Truth.

I liken Bethlehemjudah to the Church of today and what a blessing it is to dwell in the house of God! When I walk through the doors of my church, I thank the Lord for His wonderful presence and abundant blessing in my life. During my darkest hours, as I travelled the deserts of despair and forests of frustration, I found protection and peace when I entered into my church. Each church service became my sanctuary from the punishing blows everyday life landed on my spirit.

When we meet Elimelech and Naomi, they were living in the midst of a twenty year famine in the land of Bethlehemjudah that had the people in a paralyzing grip of hunger and despair. The word *famine* is used to mirror the image of the physical condition of the dry, parched, unproductive land to the spiritual condition of its people.

With no relief in sight, Elimelech decided to move his wife and sons out of Judah and away from the people of God into the godless country of Moab. The plan was to stay a short while until the trouble at home was finished and then go back home. Unfortunately, even the best laid plans can go very wrong.

When Naomi followed her husband out of the sanctuary of Bethlehem, it was an act of turning away from the Lord and toward a world of sin. Moab was a nation known for its worship of Baal, Ashtoreth and Chemoth; the Canaanite gods of fertility and agriculture. The religious rituals of the nation included human, specifically, child sacrifice by fire and offering sacrificial virgins to the priests at the temples.

"Thou shalt fear the LORD thy God, and serve him, and shalt swear

by his name. Ye shall not go after other gods, of the gods of the people

which are round about you; (For the LORD thy God is a jealous God

among you) lest the anger of the LORD thy God be kindled against

thee, and destroy thee from off the face of the earth."

Deuteronomy 6:13-15

It is not surprising that Naomi would follow her charismatic husband, for Elimelech's name means *"god-like one, mighty one, angels, god, false god, demons, imaginations."* According to his name, Elemelech was persuasive, arrogant and filled with a "god-like" tendency which is a sense of self that places him above others, including the authority of God.

Naomi loved her husband, Elimelech, to distraction and worshipped the ground he walked on. He was her sunshine in the morning and the stars twinkling at night. There is nothing wrong with being head over heels in love with your husband, unless you journey the path of Naomi, and make him the god of your life, too.

When the love of her life died, Naomi was left with two sons to rear on her own, and was free to leave Moab. Instead of packing up her children and returning to the support and safety of family and the house of God, she chose to stay in the land of false gods. Naomi's sons grew up in a godless atmosphere and ended up marrying the Moabite women, Orpah and Ruth. Soon, her son, Mahlon died, and then, she lost Chilion. Still, Naomi remained in Moab on her own accord; it was *her choice to stay.*

The Scripture says nothing about Naomi serving the Lord or being a woman of faith during her sojourn in Moab. It never mentions her seeking the Lord in any way, or taking responsibility for her actions and bad choices. The Scripture does record Naomi blaming God for allowing her husband and sons to die; therefore, leaving her and her daughter-in-laws alone.

> *...for it grieveth me much for your sakes that*
> *the hand of the LORD is gone out against me.*
> Ruth 1:13

If Naomi had chosen to serve the Lord and be a light of Truth to her family, the dynamic of her situation would have been changed on multiple levels. Her husband would have experienced God through her. The Lord would have used her in an area of ministry. What if Naomi had changed the climate of her spirit and orchestrated an atmosphere of joy, praise and peace in her home?

I cannot say that Naomi would have been spared the terrible events that took place. But, I am able to say, with all confidence, that God would have gladly been Naomi's hope and comfort. He was waiting to be her shield and buckler, her refuge and strength. Our Lord *desires* to carry us through the hard times in our lives.

None of the heartbreaking experiences in Naomi's life led her to repentance. She was content to stay in Moab, surrounded by false gods and their rituals. Finally, Naomi was desolate. She had *nothing* left; no husband, no sons, no money, no income and no way of making any money. Then, when she heard that the Lord had visited Bethlehemjudah, she began to make plans to go back to her home.

> *...for she had heard in the country of Moab how that*
> *the LORD had visited his people in giving them bread.*
> Ruth 1:6

I believe Naomi maintained a religious standard in regards to her faith in the Lord. Perhaps, she did this by dressing the part of a Hebrew, talking about the "old days" before the years of famine, or staunchly (and self-righteously) proclaiming the mighty works of the one true God. Whatever Naomi did, it was not enough to maintain a secure walk with Him. Yet, somewhere, somehow, in the midst of Naomi's imperfect example, Ruth heard the salvation message.

> *And Ruth said, Intreat me not to leave thee, or to*
> *return from following after thee: for whither thou*
> *goest, I will go; and where thou lodgest, I will lodge:*
> *thy people shall be my people, and thy God my God*
> *Ruth 1:16*

It is a sad state of affairs, when a person who has access to the Almighty God, His love, mercy and grace, chooses to remain cold, bitter and dead on the inside. In other words, we may know the gospel, but, not love it. We can take someone to church, lead them to Christ, and be left needing salvation ourselves. Ruth is proof that God is able to use anyone, with any attitude, to reach a hungry soul.

> *"So they two went until they came to Bethlehem. And it*
> *came to pass, when they were come to Bethlehem, that*
> *all the city was moved about them, and they said, Is this*
> *Naomi? And she said unto them, Call me not Naomi, call*
> *me Mara: for the Almighty hath dealt very bitterly with me.*
> *I went out full and the LORD hath brought me home again*
> *empty: why then call ye me Naomi, seeing the LORD hath*
> *testified against me, and the Almighty hath afflicted me?"*
> *Ruth 1:19-21*

Last week, my Pastor taught on two styles of learning: the easy way, by instruction, or the hard way, through experience. Instruction is an easy tutor, bestowing eager students with an immediate knowledge base from a stockpile of wisdom and lesson plans. Experience is a hard taskmaster whose education is slow, grueling and very thorough by challenging hard nosed students through a string of events, until the lessons are learned.

EXPERIENCE IS NOT ALWAYS THE KINDEST OF TEACHERS, BUT IT IS SURELY THE BEST
~Spanish Proverb

Have you ever asked yourself, "Why do I always come back to this place in my life?" or "Why does this always happen to me?" If you're like me, you already know the answer: there is a lesson to be learned, and I'm not catching on. I wish I could tell you that I have always been a quick study, but I cannot. In fact, it was not until I fell flat on my face several times, that I realized there was an easier way to learn: such as listening to the teacher and heeding their instruction.

One of my hard lessons with Rich was in the differences of our parenting styles. I have a structured style, using chore charts, schedules and making my children responsible and accountable for accomplishing each goal. I expect to know where they are, who they are with, and when they will be home. Rich, on the other hand, is my polar opposite and never will our two trains meet!

For years, I would badger Rich and try to teach him how to be a *good and responsible* parent. Every time his boys 'disappeared', I would be frantic, because I did not know where they were, when they would be home, and neither did Rich. It infuriated me that he did not seem to care or understand why I did. When I verbalized my angst with the situation, my husband just looked at me, confused by my reaction and upset by my lack of confidence in him. During that time, my flesh was in control when I responded to my husband. Jesus had nothing to do with it and it showed.

It took me *several* times around to this point to learn

that being a control freak with Rich was not a good **thing**, and did not produce a peaceful, Christ-filled atmosphere in my home. Now, after much practice and *much prayer*, I choose to have faith in God to keep my mouth shut, use common sense and wisdom as I quietly back away from Rich's parenting decisions. And, you know what? Our kids have all turned out just fine. Total opposites, but, *great kids*, all the same!

In a perfect world, there is no hunger, no worries, and everyone lives happily ever after. But, reality is a myriad of messy choices, sad turns of events and happy accidents. As Christians, we live in the thick of reality, because, every morning we are asked, "Who will you serve?" and we make an eternal choice, whether we say anything, or not.

Naomi made a choice everyday *not to grow* and prosper in the Spirit. Even the deaths of her husband and sons could not reach into Naomi's heart, and convince her to change her way of living. When Naomi returned from Moab, she asked people to call her *"Mara"* or *"Bitter."* Her declaration of bitterness shows each and every one of us what will happen if we turn from serving the Lord, to serving man. She refused to learn the lessons set before her that could have saved her from being filled with bitterness and shame.

In the book of Ruth, we met Naomi who gives us a mad dose of reality, one reality check at a time. She was a godly woman who followed her man into a world of sin. Her priorities got skewed and her commitment to the Lord got lost in the reality of everyday life. But, our God is a God of promise, mercy and grace, loving us at our most unlovable times. He is able to see into the darkest part of our hearts and save us from ourselves.

In the end, Naomi was saved from sin, secure with family and served the Lord.

IT'S TERRIBLY HARD TO BE MARRIED...
HARDER THAN ANYTHING ELSE.
I THINK YOU HAVE TO BE AN ANGEL.
~August Strindberg,
A Dream Play

LIONS, TROPHIES AND LIFE...
OH, MY!

"Be sober, be vigilant; because your adversary the devil, as a roaring lion, walketh about, seeking whom he may devour: Whom resist stedfast in the faith, knowing that the same afflictions are accomplished in your brethren that are in the world. But the God of all grace, who hath called us unto his eternal glory by Christ Jesus, after that ye have suffered a while, make you perfect, stablish, strengthen, settle you."

1 Peter 5:8-10

The real battle raging in your home is a nefarious throw down over *your salvation!* It is the prize of destroying you that is on the line, and *your* head that is at risk of being made a trophy on Hell's Wall of Fame.

If Satan succeeds in his trickery, it will not only affect those you influence, but, he will achieve his ultimate goal of insuring that **you** — *the daughter of The King* — will be lost. He will utilize any and all tactics in which to destroy those who serve God and to prevent as many as possible from coming to the knowledge of Truth.

Since the devil is like a roaring lion, *seeking to devour someone*, it won't be one of his own he's seeking, but, a specific delectable morsel for his insatiable and diabolical hunger: *you.* The battle we are engaged in reaches much farther than our husbands' salvation! The enemy of our souls seeks to devour us and steal the eternal promise of Christ.

A lion does not hunt, kill or eat other lions. They seek

out other animals, typically herds, which will feed many members of their household, or 'pride', for some time. Lions have two distinctive styles of hunting. The first is most common in which the lion will stalk its' prey from cover to cover, then, strikes with a final burst of speed. The second form of hunting is to find a bush close to something their prey needs, such as water, climb in and wait.

The actual lions' hunt is an extremely organized team effort. A larger group of lionesses will lay in wait, hiding downwind of the targeted herd, while another lioness moves stealthily around the herd until she is upwind of it. She abruptly breaks cover, separates one animal from the herd and kills it. This startles the remaining herd, which chases them straight towards the hidden lionesses and their demise.

Hells intention is to wear us down and distort the blessed promise of our salvation into a cursed millstone of despair. Then, at our weakest time, the enemy of our soul will attack and devour us, sending our family running into the hidden traps he has set for them. Remember, there are two major skills lions have that guarantee an effective and efficient hunt: they are extraordinarily adept at hiding and phenomenally patient.

"I make a decree, That in every dominion of my kingdom
men tremble and fear before the God of Daniel: for he
is the living God, and stedfast for ever, and his kingdom
that which shall not be destroyed, and his dominion shall
be even unto the end. He delivereth and rescueth, and he
worketh signs and wonders in heaven and in earth, who
hath delivered Daniel from the power of the lions."

Daniel 6:26-27

Sometimes, living with an unsaved husband can feel like we have been thrown into a lion's den, but, just as God closed the mouths of the lions for Daniel, he will also do for us. He will do this because He has a specific call on our lives, a ministry that we will excel in, and certain people that only we can reach! Jesus Christ is the only guarantee we have for success in this life, and He is the only Hope for our husband's salvation. Our faithful service to God maintains an open door of opportunity for our husbands, allowing them to experience Christ every day through us!

Three of the women we have met during our time together changed the course of humanity, served the Lord with great vigor, raised armies, raised disciples, saved homes and households *because they were married to particular men.* Their focus was God-ward and not on the fact that their husbands were not serving the Most High. Service to God was the richest part of their life, each and every day.

No matter what came their way, Deborah, Abigail and Eunice remained faithful and constant in their service to the Lord, and He blessed them with great ministry. God hand-picked these women to accomplish the task set before them by God. Were they the only ones who would answer the call to perform them? Maybe.

Think about Naomi. She is our example of a woman who allowed her circumstance to circumvent her service to the Lord. Many times, I have heard it preached that if we will not do what God asks of us; He will find someone who will, and He did with Ruth!

Far be it from me to allow anyone else to take on my tasks, perform my praise and assume the responsibility that the Lord desires for my life. I will not cave into feelings of inadequacy. I refuse to accept the lie of the enemy that tells me I am "less" of a Christian because my husband does not serve the Lord.

I will not let my King down, I will not allow someone else do the job that the Lord has specifically chosen for me to do. Who am I to deny the Lord His perfect will? I will not slam the door of ministry into the face of God; I must courageously walk through it and follow the path laid out for me.

That is why I am here today, sitting here at my laptop fighting to write these words. I am here to encourage you, my dear sister, to join me in this battle for your marriage and family! Embrace your marriage vows and perform them with praise and worship! Grow in Christ, fulfill your commission and bless the Lord every day for the man you are married to.

"For I am now ready to be offered, and the time of my departure is at hand. I have fought a good fight, I have finished my course, I have kept the faith: Henceforth there is laid up for me a crown of righteousness, which the Lord, the righteous judge, shall give me at that day: and not to me only, but unto all them also that love his appearing."

2 Timothy 4:6-8

You and I fight the good fight and share the battle with many women that we will never know, let alone meet in our lifetime. But, when we get to Heaven, all of us will be there, and we will be victorious and dancing on streets of gold! Together, we will throw our crowns at the altar of Christ, like graduates at the end of commencement ceremony.

I sit here at my laptop and wonder, how can I possibly impart to you the value that the Lord places on you, personally? I want to send you on your way, enlightened, empowered and refreshed with a new sense of direction and purpose in your life.

You will always have my prayers and my undying respect. I love you for who you are, where you are going and the service to the Lord that you sacrificially give and show as witness to your husband. If anything I have said has helped you grow and blossom in our dear Father's kingdom, then I can close my laptop and walk away with joy in my heart, being blessed in having shared this time with you.

I am waiting for the day that we can be together, with the tears forgotten, the dancing shoes on and enjoy lively fellowship at the Dinner of the Lamb.

Grace be unto you, and peace, from God our Father, and from the Lord Jesus Christ. I thank my God upon every remembrance of you, Always in every prayer of mine for you all making request with joy.

Philippians 1:2-4

REFERENCES

Burkert, Walter. *Greek Religion*. Boston: Harvard UP, 1987.

Cook, David C. *10. The Bible Knowledge Commentary: Old Testament*. Colorado Springs: David C. Cook, 1993.

Doty, Lynda Allison. *Apostolic Counseling*. Kearney: Morris, 2000.

Jacobs, Rabbi Louis. "The Jewish Religion: A Companion. 1995. <http://www.myjewishlearning.com>.

Kachelman, Jr, John L. "Timothy, A Man of Character." 1998.

Kirkpatrick, Alexander F. *The First Book of Samuel: With Map, Notes and Introduction*. Cambridge: Cambridge UP, 1889.

Metzger, Bruce M., and Michael D. Coogan. *The Oxford Companion to the Bible*. Oxford UP: Oxford, 1993.

Orr M.A., D.D., James. "Definition for EUNICE." International Standard Bible Encyclopedia. 1915. <www. bible-history.com>.

Schauss, Hayyim. "The Evolution of Marriage: Ancient Jewish Marriage." n.d. <http://www.myjewishlearning.com>.

Strong, James. *Strong's Exhaustive Concordance of the Bible*. Nashville: Thomas Nelson, 1990.